TURBO the FLYING DOG

This book is dedicated
to all the people and paws
that make our lives complete.

Published in 2015 by 8 Paws Press
Maryland

Copyright © 2015 8 Paws Press

ISBN 978-1-942593-02-7

Today was the day. Turbo was finally going to learn to fly!

Once a lonely shelter dog, Turbo now had a family.
They flew him home in an airplane.

He was scared at first, but not anymore. His mom and dad are pilots, and now he was going to flight school!

Turbo bounded into the flight school. "I am here to learn to fly!"
he squealed to the chihuahua at the front desk.

"I'm sorry, we only have a girl instructor here today. Girl pilots are not as good as boy pilots," the chihuahua replied.

"That's ok," Turbo said, wondering what was wrong with a girl pilot.
Soon a curly haired black dog trotted up and smiled at him.
"Hi, my name is Olive," she said.

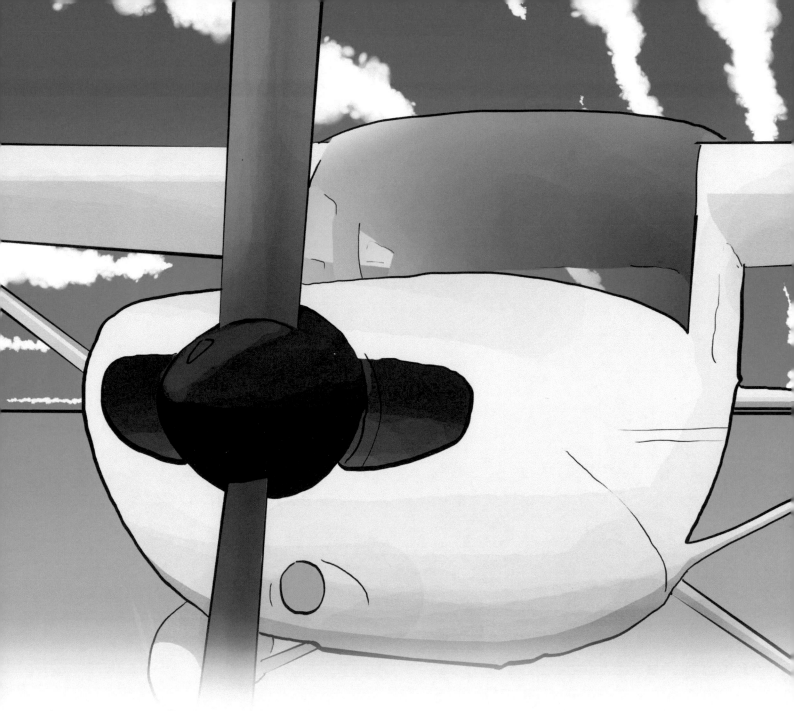

Olive took Turbo outside to the airplane. "First we need to make sure the plane is safe to fly. This is called a pre-flight," she explained. "This is the propeller." Olive pointed to it. "It spins and makes the plane move forward."

Next, Olive showed Turbo the ailerons. They move up and down and make the plane turn. "The pilot controls them from inside the plane with the yoke," Olive told Turbo.

"This is the elevator," Olive said. "It makes the plane go up and down. You control it with the yoke, too."

"Everything is working! It's time to fly!" Olive barked.
Both dogs climbed into the plane.

Turbo's eyes lit up and he reached for the controls.
"Seatbelts first!" Olive yapped.

Once the seat belts went click, Olive taught Turbo how to drive an airplane on the ground.

"This is called taxiing," Olive said. "You put your feet on the rudder pedals to steer."

Turbo and Olive taxied to the runway where they prepared for takeoff.

"Bark, bark and away!" Turbo howled gleefully as they sped into the sky.

"You're a good pilot," Turbo told Olive as they soared above the clouds.

"A lot of people think I shouldn't be a pilot because I'm a girl," Olive said. She was frowning.

"That doesn't mean you can't be a good pilot," Turbo said.
"My mom is a pilot and she's great at flying!"

"Really?" asked Olive. "Does she get teased?"

"Sometimes she does," Turbo told Olive. "But there are lots of great girl pilots! There is no difference as long as you practice, right?"

Olive smiled. "You're right! You are a good friend, Turbo.
Come on, I'll show you how to turn!"

"If you turn the yoke left, the plane turns left. Now you try!"

"Oh, I've got it!" Turbo said as Olive handed him the controls.
"If I turn the yoke right the plane will go right!"

His lesson went by very fast. Before Turbo knew it,
Olive told him it was time to land.

Turbo looked at the earth below him and
enjoyed the view a moment longer.

"You can land the plane," offered Olive.
"You did a great job flying today!"

Turbo pushed down on the yoke and came in for a smooth landing.

As they climbed out of the plane, the chihuahua was waiting.

"Sorry Turbo," she said. "You can have a boy instructor next time."

"Turbo knows girls can fly just as well as boys! You're a girl, we should support each other!" Olive told the chihuahua. She held her head high.

"Olive, I'll fly with you anytime!" exclaimed Turbo. "Let's fly again!"

Turbo and Olive flew off toward their next adventure.
"Bark, bark and away!" they yelled.

48904656R00021

Made in the USA
Charleston, SC
15 November 2015